CU00704527

WE'RE TALKING ABOUT
VEGETARIANISM

SAMANTHA CALVERT

WAYLAND

WRITHLINGTON SCHOOL
LEARNING RESOURCE
CENTRE

Editor: Carron Brown
Series Designer: John Christopher
Designer: Malcolm Walker, Kudos Design

First published in 1997 by Wayland Publishers Ltd
61 Western Road, Hove, East Sussex, BN3 1JD, England

© Copyright 1997 Wayland Publishers Ltd

British Library Cataloguing in Publication Data
Calvert, Samantha
We're Talking About Vegetarianism
1. Vegetarianism – Juvenile literature 2. Vegetarian children
– Juvenile literature 3. Vegetarian cookery – Juvenile literature
I. Title II. Vegetarianism
613.2 ' 62

ISBN 0 7502 2031 7

Typeset by Malcolm Walker, Kudos Design, England
Printed and bound by Canale & C.S.p.A, Turin, Italy

Picture Acknowledgements
Cephas 5, 29; Chapel Studios 24; Ecoscene 10, 11, 14; Eye Ubiquitous
6, 28, /James Davis Travel Photography 17; Life File 7; Popperfoto 17;
Zak Waters cover, title page, 4, 8, 10, 12, 13, 16, 20, 23; Wayland
Picture Library 9, 14, 15, 18, 19, 21, 22, 25, 26, 27.
The illustration on page 19 is by John Yates.

Photo shoots directed by Bridget Tily.
Thank you to all the children who posed as models for this book.
Most of the people photographed in this book are models.

Contents

Finding out about vegetarianism

Sarah asked Marie to her house for dinner. She knew Marie was one of the people in her class who was vegetarian. Sarah wanted to know what foods Marie liked to eat. She asked Marie to tell her more about vegetarianism.

Marie explained that vegetarians eat much the same food as anyone else. They eat fruit and vegetables, nuts and seeds, beans and pulses, milk, cheese, yoghurt, cream and free-range eggs. The only difference is that vegetarians are people who don't eat meat: including steak, pork, poultry, fish and shellfish. Vegetarians also try not to eat foods that are made using other parts of animals, such as gelatine, found in some sweets and jellies.

▶ Sarah asked Marie about vegetarianism on the way home from school.

There are many different types of vegetarian:

1) Some vegetarians eat eggs and dairy products as well as other vegetarian foods such as fruit and vegetables. They are known as OVO-LACTO-VEGETARIANS.

2) Some vegetarians don't eat eggs but do eat dairy products as well as other vegetarian foods. They are known as LACTO-VEGETARIANS.

3) Some vegetarians don't eat dairy products but eat eggs as well as other vegetarian foods. They as known as OVO-VEGETARIANS.

4) Some vegetarians don't eat eggs or dairy products, but eat only strict vegetarian foods that do not contain any products to do with animals. These people are known as VEGANS.

5) Some people don't eat red meat but eat chicken, fish, eggs and dairy products as well as vegetarian food. They are trying to cut down on having meat in their diets. These people are known as DEMI-VEGETARIANS.

◀ Vegetarians eat many different foods, not just vegetables.

You may have already heard a great deal about vegetarianism. Some of the things you have been told may be out-of-date, others may simply be incorrect. This book will help you find out more about vegetarianism and to make up your own mind about what you think about it.

The word 'vegetarian' was first chosen in 1847 to describe the diet of the people who set up the first Vegetarian Society in Great Britain. Many people think the word 'vegetarian' comes from the word 'vegetable'. In fact, it comes from the Latin word 'vegetus' meaning 'lively'. The group of people who chose the word thought 'lively' described how their diet made them feel.

Why do people become vegetarians?

There are many different reasons for becoming a vegetarian. Many people who make the decision to become vegetarians are under 19 years old. In the early 1990s, it became more common for young people between 11 and 13 years old to become vegetarian[1]. There are many different reasons why people choose not to eat meat. These include cruelty to farm animals and pollution of the countryside and seas. Some of these reasons are explained later in this book.

Some people are vegetarian because they are born into a vegetarian family and have been brought up on a vegetarian diet. These people are sometimes called life vegetarians. As more adult vegetarians have families, life vegetarians are becoming more common.

▼ Many young people become vegetarians.

Some families are vegetarian because of their religious beliefs. Many of the world's religions encourage people not to eat meat because they believe that it is wrong to kill animals. For example, many Hindus and Buddhists do not eat meat.

Many people in the world do not have any choice but to be vegetarian. In some poorer countries, people cannot afford to eat meat, so they eat cheaper foods such as rice or wheat.

▼ Many Buddhists do not eat meat.

Imran's story

Imran has been a vegetarian for three years. He became a vegetarian because he did not like the idea of eating animals.

Imran has two pet dogs who he looks after well. He takes the dogs out for long walks, brushes them regularly and feeds them. He cannot imagine hurting them. He would not like to hurt any animal.

Imran watched a programme on television about how the animals on some farms are kept in cruel conditions. Some farms keep hens in small cages, called battery cages. Each hen has a very small space to live in, where they cannot move around or stretch their wings. They have no sunlight or fresh air. Their feathers can be plucked out by other angry, bored hens and their feet can be damaged by standing for a long time on the wire floors of their cages.

Some farms keep pigs in narrow, metal crates where they cannot turn around or move backwards or forwards. Other farm animals can suffer too.

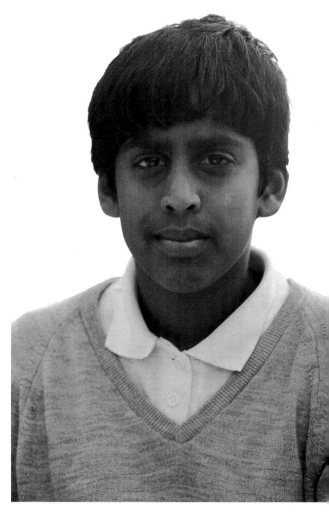

▲ Imran has been a vegetarian for three years because he loves animals.

8

▶ This sheep and her lamb are inside so that they will not catch cold. Some sheep are kept in spaces smaller than this one for most of their lives.

Imran realized that these animals were just like his pet dogs. They felt pain and knew what it was like to be afraid. He thought he could help them by not eating chickens or pigs or any other animals.

Animals kept in crowded conditions are intensively farmed. Intensive farming means that many animals are kept in small spaces so they can be easily controlled by the farmers. Kept in this way, with special diets, the animals grow faster, have more young, grow more wool or produce more milk than they would naturally. This is the cheapest way of keeping animals. It means that meat, eggs and milk are cheap to buy. Some farm animals are less intensively farmed and may lead better lives.

Did you know that ...
During their lifetime the average British meat-eater will consume 36 pigs, 36 sheep, 8 cows and 550 poultry. The average fish eater will consume over 500 kg of fish[2].

Jane's story

Jane has always been very concerned about the environment. She felt that as well as recycling and buying environmentally friendly products, she could also help by changing her diet.

Jane read an article in a magazine that explained about animal farming. Animal farming uses more water than plant crops because animals need to drink water and farmers need water for the crops to feed the animals. A pound of wheat can be grown with 113 litres of water, but up

▲ Jane read an article about animal farming.

to 11,250 litres is needed to produce a pound of meat[3]. Some countries find it very difficult to get water supplies to produce their food.

Millions of tonnes of animal slurry from farmed animals are produced each year. Animal slurry is a hundred times more polluting than human sewage[4]. This sewage is stored in tanks on farms and, if it leaks into rivers or streams, it can kill fish and pollute the water.

◄ Less water is used to grow wheat than to produce meat.

▲ Animal sewage can cause harm to the environment.

Jane also read that in other countries, large areas of rain forest are being cleared to make room for cattle ranches, which produce meat for the USA beefburger trade. In some areas of South America, cattle ranching is responsible for up to 50 per cent of all tropical rain forest destruction. An area of rain forest the size of Wales is destroyed every year[5].

The seas are also affected. Eight of the world's major fishing grounds have been overfished and nine others are in danger[6]. Stocks of fish have fallen so low that many countries now limit how many fish can be caught. In the North Sea, one-quarter of the entire fish population is caught every year. Half of the fish caught will be made into fertilizer or animal food.

Becoming a vegetarian

When Lucy wanted to become a vegetarian, her parents were not pleased. Her mum said that Lucy would not be able to get all the vitamins and minerals that she needed to stay healthy on a vegetarian diet. Her dad said it was just a silly 'phase' that she would grow out of. They did not want to have to buy different foods for Lucy and cook two meals all the time. Her parents thought that Lucy's new diet would cause a lot of work for them.

However, Lucy really wanted to be a vegetarian. So she went to the library and borrowed books about eating healthily and some vegetarian cook books. She also wrote to The Vegetarian Society and asked them for more information.

▲ Lucy wrote away for more information about vegetarianism. She wanted to make sure that she would be eating enough of the right foods to be healthy.

▶ Lucy's mum and dad also read the information sent by The Vegetarian Society to try and understand Lucy's decision to become a vegetarian.

Lucy showed all this information to her mum and dad. She tried to explain to them why she wanted to be a vegetarian, being careful not to get angry or shout. Her parents saw that Lucy was serious about becoming a vegetarian and that she was trying hard to find all the right information. They could see that being vegetarian meant a great deal to Lucy. So they agreed that she could become a vegetarian. In return, Lucy agreed to help her mum and dad with the shopping and cooking.

When Lucy became a vegetarian, her friends did not understand her decision. At school, they waved meat under her nose and asked her to try some. Sometimes, during lunch break, they would throw meat into her sandwich box. However, some of Lucy's friends told her that they admired the decision that she had made. Some decided to become vegetarians too.

What do vegetarians eat?

If you have always eaten a meat-based diet, it can be difficult to imagine what a vegetarian could eat. Just vegetables? That would not be very interesting. What about people who don't like the taste of vegetables? Could they be vegetarians? What would they eat?

A typical meal for someone who eats meat might be some meat with potatoes and another vegetable. Vegetarians don't just 'leave meat off the plate'. This would not be a very healthy diet. Vegetarians have to change the way they eat.

▲ Pulses are good sources of protein.

Vegetarians have a wide variety of foods to choose from. Of course, vegetarians do eat lots of fresh fruits and vegetables. But there are also three other groups of foods from which vegetarians choose things to eat. The chart on the opposite page explains these new food groups, gives some examples of the types of foods in each group and explains what essential nutrients they provide.

Vegetarians also need to include small amounts of plant oils, margarine or butter to provide energy, essential fatty acids and vitamins A, D and E.

◄ Vegetarians should eat plenty of fresh fruit and vegetables.

These ingredients can be used to make many delicious meals which are very healthy:

Group 1: cereals and grains – bread, pasta, rice, breakfast cereals. Provides: energy, fibre, B vitamins, calcium and iron.

Group 2: pulses, nuts and seeds – baked beans, kidney beans, chickpeas, all kinds of nuts, sunflower seeds, sesame seeds. Provides: protein, energy, fibre, calcium, iron and zinc.

Group 3: fruit and vegetables – a lot of apples, oranges, pears, bananas, broccoli, carrots, peppers, onions, potatoes, tomatoes, spring greens, parsnips, dried fruit. Provides: calcium, iron, folate, beta-carotene, vitamin C and fibre.

Group 4: soya and dairy products – tofu, textured soya protein (TVP), soya milk, cow's milk, cheese, yoghurt. Provides: protein, energy, calcium, minerals, vitamin B12 and vitamin D.

Marie's story

▲ Marie eats all the right vegetarian foods she needs to be healthy. Her diet includes vegetables and fruit, pasta, beans, rice and soya products.

This is Marie. She became a vegetarian a year ago. Marie became a vegetarian because she was concerned about her health. She wanted to lead a long and healthy life. Marie's friend, Sally, told her that vegetarians who have well-balanced diets are often healthier than people who eat meat. Sally explained that a vegetarian diet with a lot of fresh fruit, vegetables, pulses and cereals, and not too much cheese and milk would be very healthy.

Many people worry that vegetarians don't eat enough of the right foods to stay healthy. Every person needs a certain amount of nutrients in their bodies. A vegetarian diet should be well-planned to make sure that the body is receiving enough of each nutrient. Marie was concerned that she might be missing some nutrients by cutting meat out of her diet, so she asked her doctor what she should do. He helped her find a dietician who helped Marie plan a balanced, healthy vegetarian diet. Vegetarian diets can be very healthy for your body, but only if enough of the right foods are eaten.

Vegetarians are as strong and as energetic as meat eaters. Many champion athletes are vegetarian, such as the tennis star Martina Navratalova and the Olympic champion sprinter Carl Lewis. The foods that give you a lot of energy, such as beans, rice, bread, pasta and nuts, are all vegetarian. Many strong animals, such as gorillas and elephants, are vegetarians!

▲ Carl Lewis, the American athlete, has won many gold medals for running and long jump events.

◀ Elephants are strong and vegetarian.

What foods does your body need to be healthy?

Vegetarianism is a healthy choice, but it is very important to have a well-balanced diet. A person could eat chips and chocolate at every meal and be a vegetarian, but it would not be good for their health.

To be healthy as a vegetarian it is important to try and eat something from each of the food groups mentioned on page 15 every day.

People don't force themselves to eat food they don't like. Let's say a vegetarian hated vegetables. They could try eating some new vegetables, perhaps in a sauce or soup. If they still could not bear to eat vegetables, they would need to find other foods that contain the same nutrients.

▼ Beans and pulses are good alternatives to meat and fish.

For example, green leafy vegetables are a good source of iron, but so are breakfast cereals, chickpeas, veggie burgers, apricots, baked beans and wholewheat bread.

A varied vegetarian diet will supply all the essential nutrients needed to be fit and healthy. To be healthy, people need to eat protein, carbohydrate, fat, vitamins and minerals, and some fibre.

The plate on the right shows what types of foods should be eaten, and in what quantities. Oil, butter and other fats, for example, are the smallest section because we only need small amounts of these. Bread, other cereals, potatoes and fruit and vegetables are the largest sections because we should eat these in the greatest quantities.

Source: *The Balance of Good Health* published by the Department of Health.

Fruit and vegetables – choose many different types.
Bread, other cereals and potatoes – eat all types and choose high-fibre kinds whenever possible.
Alternatives to meat and fish, such as TVP and tofu – choose lower-fat alternatives whenever possible.
Fatty and sugary foods – try not to eat these too often, and when you do, have small amounts.
Milk, dairy foods and alternatives – choose lower fat alternatives whenever possible.

The hidden foods vegetarians avoid

When Imran first became a vegetarian, he was invited to Helen's birthday party. At the party, Imran's friend, Matt, told him that he could not eat the jelly and some of the cakes because he was a vegetarian. Imran did not believe him. Matt explained that some jellies contain gelatine, which is made from boiled-down animal skin and bones. Imran decided to contact The Vegetarian Society in case there were other hidden foods vegetarians should not eat.

The Vegetarian Society sent some information to Imran. They told him that there were many ingredients that make up foods which are unsuitable for vegetarians, such as animal fat which can be found in cakes, biscuits, bread and desserts.

Whey comes from the cheese-making process. If the cheese is

▲ Matt pointed out to Imran that jelly was not vegetarian.

suitable for vegetarians, then the whey is too. If the cheese is made with animal rennet, the whey is not suitable for vegetarians. Whey is found in margarine, cakes and biscuits. Vegetarians avoid whey unless the packet says 'suitable for vegetarians'.

Some E numbers may not be suitable for vegetarians. For example, E120 is made from crushed insects. E numbers are found in many ready-made foods and sweets.

Many of the foods Imran thought were vegetarian were not really vegetarian. He learned that the best way to make sure food was suitable for his new diet was to look for the words 'suitable for vegetarians', or The Vegetarian Society's ❤ symbol. Imran decided to make changes slowly so that he could learn which foods were not suitable for his new diet. It is a good idea for new vegetarians to think carefully about these changes and make them slowly. Remember, even people who have been vegetarians for years still make mistakes and eat foods with these hidden products in them.

▼ Some sweets can contain gelatine and are not vegetarian.

Try exciting new foods

When Lucy became a vegetarian some of her friends asked her what she would eat. 'If you take away meat, chicken and fish, you're just left with vegetables', they said. In the end, Lucy's mum and dad were very helpful in her change over to vegetarianism. They visited their local health-food store and supermarkets, and found many new types of food for her to try.

Lucy discovered that there were many types of beans. Not just baked beans, green beans and broad beans, but aduki beans, black-eyed beans, butter beans, soya beans, chickpeas and kidney beans. She found buying the beans in cans helped to cut down on the time taken to soak and cook them.

▼ There are many different types of beans.

Lentils also come in many different varieties. The most common are red, green and brown. Lucy uses them to make spaghetti sauces, shepherd's pie or curries.

Nuts can be cooked as well as eaten dry-roasted or salted. Lucy puts them on top of dishes that are going to be baked (such as a shepherd's pie) or in salads. Peanut butter is useful for sandwiches and for adding to stews and casseroles.

▲ Lucy and her parents found many different vegetarian foods to buy.

Lucy also found many different types of seeds. Spice seeds, such as cumin, coriander, caraway and poppy seeds, are used in very small amounts to add flavour to food. Other seeds include pumpkin, sunflower and sesame seeds. Lucy's mum uses them in biscuits and salads, or on top of bakes. A few sunflower seeds roasted with some soya sauce make a delicious, healthy treat.

Tofu is a new food that Lucy discovered she could eat. Tofu is a very healthy food made from soya beans. It can be used in many different ways. Tofu can be bought in supermarkets and health-food shops. Lucy has learned that she can use it to

▲ Lucy discovered many new foods to eat, such as this Chinese stir-fry with bean sprouts and vegetables.

make both sweet and savoury dishes. Tofu can be used to make desserts such as tofu cheesecakes, as well as tofu bakes and quiches.

Another vegetarian food is Textured Vegetable Protein (TVP), also sometimes called Textured Soya Protein (TSP). It is made to replace meat in traditional dishes. Lucy buys TVP in both granules and 'meat chunks', and adds it to her favourite recipes to replace meat. TVP can be bought from supermarkets and health-food shops.

Lucy's friends thought that she would have fewer types of food to eat when she became a vegetarian.

They now know that she has discovered many new things to eat. Lucy thinks her diet is more exciting than when she ate meat. Lucy's parents have decided that they like some of the foods vegetarians eat and sometimes have vegetarian meals as a change to their meat diet.

▼ This picture shows some of the vegetarian foods available to buy.

What would happen to all the animals if everyone was vegetarian?

This is one of the most-asked questions concerning vegetarianism. Some people worry that if everyone was vegetarian, no more farm animals would be born because they would not be needed. Cows, sheep, chickens and pigs are all part of our world, in the same way as cats, dogs and horses. No one wants any of these animals to disappear.

If most people became vegetarian there would be fewer farm animals. Many of these animals could live more natural lives on well-managed sanctuaries, dairy farms and free-range egg farms.

▼ A pig and her piglets on a farm.

Although many people are becoming vegetarians, the change is gradual. People do not become vegetarian overnight. Animals are specially bred by farmers for people to eat. If people eat less meat, fewer animals will be bred and killed for food. The world will not be overrun with unwanted animals if people stop eating them.

However, not everyone will become vegetarian. Many people prefer to eat meat. In many cases, it is not because they don't like animals, but because they like the taste of meat. In the end, it is a decision people make by themselves. Just as vegetarians cannot be forced to eat meat, those who eat meat cannot be forced to become vegetarian.

► These chickens roam freely around this farm.

The future of vegetarianism

▲ Every week 2,000 people, including many young people, become vegetarian.

In March 1996, one person in twenty of the adult population described themselves as vegetarian. This is around 3 million people[8]. Since 1984, the numbers of vegetarians in the UK have more than doubled[9]. It is thought that the number of vegetarians will double again in the next ten years[10].

All sorts of people become vegetarians, especially young people. About 11 per cent of teenagers describe themselves as vegetarians[11].

As the number of vegetarians increases, vegetarianism is accepted by more and more people as being a normal diet. Around 40 per cent of people who eat meat now think vegetarianism is not out of the ordinary[12].

It is also becoming much easier for people to be vegetarian. Being a vegetarian twenty years ago was quite unusual, and it was difficult to eat out in restaurants or to buy special vegetarian foods. In the early 1990s, all this changed. Most restaurants now offer special vegetarian dishes. Vegetarian meals are also available in most school canteens. All the major supermarkets sell special vegetarian products such as TVP and tofu. Many also sell ready-made vegetarian dishes in their refrigerated areas.

It is good that people's decisions to become vegetarian are now respected. If you would like to find out more, you can find information about The Vegetarian Society on page 31.

▲ Vegetarian cookery is now taught in some school lessons.

Glossary

Animal fat Fat that comes from the carcass of an animal.

Dairy products Foods made from animal milk, for example, cheese, yoghurt and cream.

Diet The food and drink that a person regularly eats or drinks.

E numbers Flavours or colours that are added to food to make it taste or look better.

Fertile Land that is able to produce vegetables or fruit.

Free-range When animals are kept in natural conditions.

Gelatine (also spelt gelatin) A product made from boiled-down animal skin and bones.

Granules Small grains of a product.

Nutrients Elements in food that keep you healthy. They are divided into proteins, carbohydrates, fats, vitamins and minerals.

Pollutes Makes something dirty and unhealthy by adding something.

Rennet A product used in some cheeses. It comes from the stomach of a calf.

Sanctuaries Places where animals and birds can be protected.

Savoury Food that is not sweet, such as the main course at dinner.

Sewage Water and waste material carried off by an underground drain called a sewer.

Slurry A mixture of water and animal dung.